For Nick, of course ~ M. J.   •   *For Kes and Maggie* ~ V. W.

First published 2011 by Walker Books Ltd, 87 Vauxhall Walk, London SE11 5HJ • This edition published 2012 •
10 9 8 7 6 5 4 3 2 1 • Text © 2011 Martin Jenkins • Illustrations © 2011 Vicky White • The right of Martin
Jenkins and Vicky White to be identified as author and illustrator respectively of this work has been asserted by them
in accordance with the Copyright, Designs and Patents Act 1988. • This book has been typeset in Bembo • Printed
in China • All rights reserved. No part of this book may be reproduced, transmitted or stored in an information
retrieval system in any form or by any means, graphic, electronic or mechanical, including photocopying, taping and
recording, without prior written permission from the publisher. • British Library Cataloguing in Publication Data:
a catalogue record for the book is available from the British Library • ISBN 978-1-4063-3208-7 • **www.walker.co.uk**

This Walker book belongs to:

_____

_____

_____

Can We Save the Tiger?

Martin Jenkins *illustrated by* Vicky White

WALKER BOOKS
AND SUBSIDIARIES
LONDON · BOSTON · SYDNEY · AUCKLAND

The world's quite a big place, you know. But it's not that big, when you consider how much there is to squeeze into it.

After all, it's home not just to billions of people, but to the most amazing number of other kinds of living things too. And we're all jostling for space.

Us humans have changed the world a lot over the years, to make room for ourselves and to produce the things we need. We've turned forests into farmland, dammed rivers and built towns and cities to live in.

Some of the other animals and plants that we share the Earth with have coped with the changes very well. But some haven't.

In fact, some have coped so badly that they're not here any more.

They're extinct.

DODO *Raphus cucullatus*
Where found: *Mauritius in the Indian Ocean*
Last seen: *1665*

Which means we'll never see **a live dodo** ...

STELLER'S
SEA COW
Hydrodamalis gigas

Where found:
North Pacific Ocean

Last seen: *1768*

or a Steller's
sea cow, or a
marsupial wolf,
or a great auk,
or a broad-faced
potoroo …

MARSUPIAL WOLF
Thylacinus cynocephalus
Where found: *Tasmania*
Last seen: *1936*

BROAD-FACED POTOROO
Potorous platyops
Where found: *Australia*
Last seen: *1875*

GREAT AUK
Pinguinus impennis
Where found: *North Atlantic Ocean*
Last seen: *1852*

… or … I could go on and on.

And then there are all
those other species that are
still around, but only just.

They're in danger of becoming extinct, just like
the dodo and Steller's sea cow.

There are so many endangered species all over the
world that it's hard to pick out some special ones.

Still, I'm sure you'll all agree that tigers are
pretty special…

TIGER *Panthera tigris*

Where found: *Bangladesh, Bhutan, Cambodia, China, India, Indonesia, Laos, Malaysia, Myanmar, Nepal, Russian Federation, Thailand, Vietnam*

Size: *weighs up to 300 kg; measures up to 3.5 m long (the biggest cat in the world)*

Lifespan: *up to 20 years in zoos, usually up to 15 or so in the wild*

Habits: *usually lives in forests and sometimes in grassland, swampy areas or farmland. Lives alone (except for mothers looking after their young)*

Breeding: *normally two to four cubs are born. Only the mother looks after them. They stay with her until they are about two years old*

Eats: *other animals. Usually hunts at night*

Number left: *fewer than 2,500 breeding adults in the wild*

Tigers are big and they're beautiful and they're fierce. And all this makes life difficult for them these days.

Because **they're big** they need a lot of space. But the countries where they live, like India and Indonesia, have huge numbers of people in them too, all trying to make a living and all needing to be fed.

And because **they're beautiful**, people have always hunted them for their skins. They also kill them for their bones and meat to use as medicines.

And because **tigers are fierce**, they don't mix very well with humans. They usually eat deer and antelope and other wild animals, but when there are people nearby, they may end up eating farm animals like cows, sheep and goats instead. Sometimes (though hardly ever), some tigers, usually old or sick ones, end up eating people too.

So if you were a poor farmer trying to make a living with a couple of cows and a few goats, you might not be too happy if you found there was a hungry tiger living nearby. And if you knew that someone might pay you more for a tiger skin and some bones than you could earn in three whole months working in the fields, then you might find it very tempting to set a trap or two, even if you knew it was against the law.

Perhaps it's not too surprising that there aren't that many tigers left.

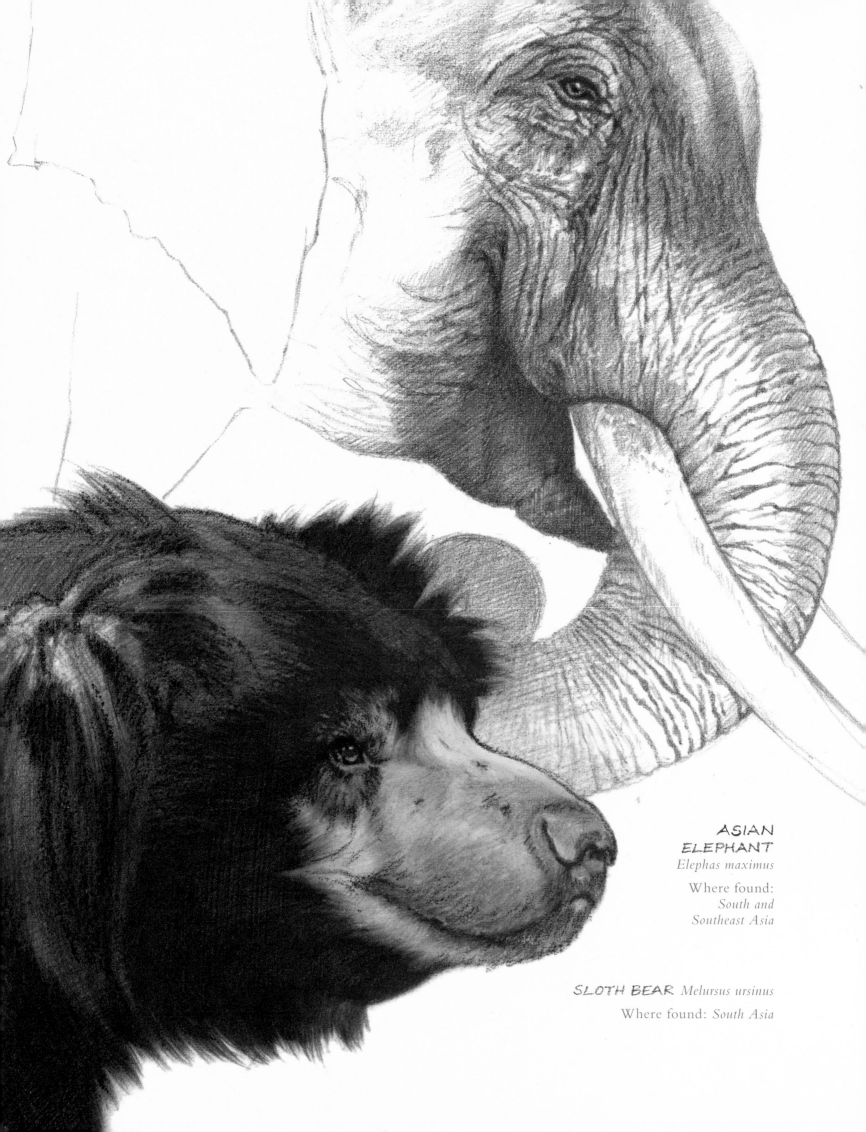

**ASIAN
ELEPHANT**
Elephas maximus

Where found:
*South and
Southeast Asia*

SLOTH BEAR *Melursus ursinus*

Where found: *South Asia*

AFRICAN
HUNTING DOG
Lycaon pictus
Where found: *Africa*

Many other animals are also running
out of room, including these ones.

Not all endangered species need lots of space.

Take partula snails. They're tiny –

so small that one of them could happily spend its whole

life in a medium-sized bush. And they're not at all scary.

But like tigers they're in big trouble, although nobody

really meant to give them a hard time.

PARTULA SNAILS *Partula (over 120 species)*

Where found: *islands in the Pacific Ocean, especially in French Polynesia where there were originally 63 species. Now only 5 of these are left in the wild and 11 others survive in zoos. The rest are extinct*

Size: *less than 2 cm long*

Lifespan: *up to five years*

Habits: *lives in trees and bushes*

Breeding: *each snail produces one live baby every six to eight weeks*

Eats: *plants*

Partula snails live on islands in the Pacific Ocean, miles from anywhere. There are lots of different kinds and they've been here for millions of years.

When the first people arrived on the islands hundreds of years ago, the partula snails didn't seem to mind too much and just got on with their lives, feeding on leaves in the forests.

Then, about a hundred years ago, people brought a different kind of snail to the islands. This was the giant African land snail.

They brought it because it's good to eat – it makes especially delicious snail soup – and is very easy to look after.

The giant African land snails rather took to the islands and soon there were loads of them, many more than anyone wanted to eat. And it turned out that they had pretty healthy appetites themselves. Soon they were chomping their way through people's crops as if there was no tomorrow.

Something had to be done.

GIANT AFRICAN LAND SNAIL *Achatina fulica*

Where found: *originally East Africa, now many different parts of the world, including Asia, South America, the West Indies and islands in the Pacific Ocean*

Unfortunately what people decided to do was to introduce a third kind of snail. This one was called the rosy euglandina and its favourite food was ... other snails.

The idea was that the rosy euglandina would feed on the giant African land snails, and stop them eating everyone's crops.

This worked a bit, but not that well – there are still plenty of the giant snails on the islands. The problem was that the rosy euglandinas found the partula snails – which weren't doing anyone any harm – the most delicious snack and quickly started eating them all up instead.

And now there are hardly any partula snails at all. Some kinds have become extinct, and some now live only in zoos and a few still hang on in places that the rosy euglandina hasn't managed to reach, yet.

ROSY EUGLANDINA
Euglandina rosea

Where found: *originally Florida, USA, now introduced to French Polynesia, New Guinea, Hawaii, the Philippines and other islands in the Pacific Ocean*

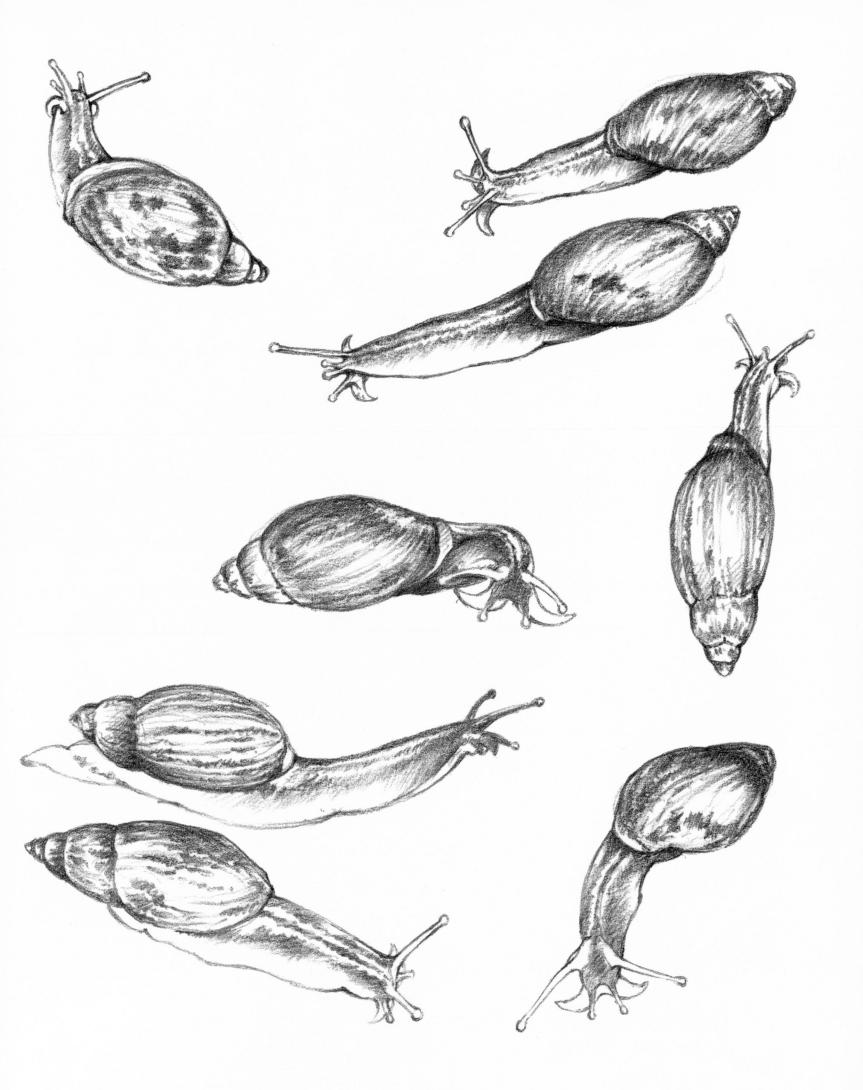

QUOKKA *Setonix brachyurus*
Where found: *Australia*
Attacked by: *foxes and cats*

MARIANA FRUIT DOVE *Ptilinopus roseicapilla*
Where found: *Mariana Islands, Pacific Ocean (now extinct on Guam)*
Attacked by: *brown tree snake*

GROUND IGUANAS *Cyclura (nine species)*
Where found: *West Indies*
Attacked by: *cats, dogs, pigs, rats and mongooses*

Other animals, including these ones, are also affected by predators that have been introduced by people.

Ugly things can be endangered too.

Perhaps I'm being unfair, but I don't think many people would call vultures exactly beautiful.

But they are definitely Very Useful Animals. They eat carrion – the bodies of animals that have already died – which means they do a very good job of keeping places clean.

WHITE-RUMPED VULTURE
Gyps bengalensis

Found in: *Bangladesh, Bhutan, Cambodia, India, Laos, Myanmar, Nepal, Pakistan, Thailand, Vietnam*

Size: *weighs up to 7.5 kg, wings measure 2 m across*

Lifespan: *up to 20 years*

Habits: *mostly lives on farmland and in cities and villages. Nests in big groups in trees or on clifftops or buildings*

Breeding: *each female lays one egg a year. The chick is fed by both its parents and stays in the nest until it is three months old*

Eats: *carrion*

Number left: *fewer than 10,000*

In India, until recently, there were millions of vultures, and they mostly fed on the bodies of cows that had died in the countryside. A while ago, people began to notice that there were a lot fewer vultures around than they remembered. But they weren't being hunted, and there were still places for them to nest and plenty of dead cows for them to eat. Then people noticed that the vultures they *did* see, perched on trees or buildings, often looked all droopy and miserable, as if they were sick. Was there some disease, like vulture-measles or flu, spreading across India?

It wasn't that, but it took some detective work to find out what the problem was: farmers were giving their cows a kind of medicine that was very poisonous to vultures. When the vultures fed on the body of a cow that had been given the medicine, they got sick and died.

Now that everyone knows what the problem is, perhaps something can be done about it. People can try to persuade the government to stop that particular medicine being sold, and can try to explain to farmers why it shouldn't be used.

But it's never as simple as that. The companies that make the medicine will lose out on the money they get from selling it, and may try to persuade the government not to do anything – who cares about a few ugly vultures, anyway? And even if it's not being made any more, there will still be lots of it about, in shops all over the country and in farmers' store-cupboards. Getting everyone everywhere to stop using it is really difficult. And by the time that's happened, it may be too late for the wild vultures.

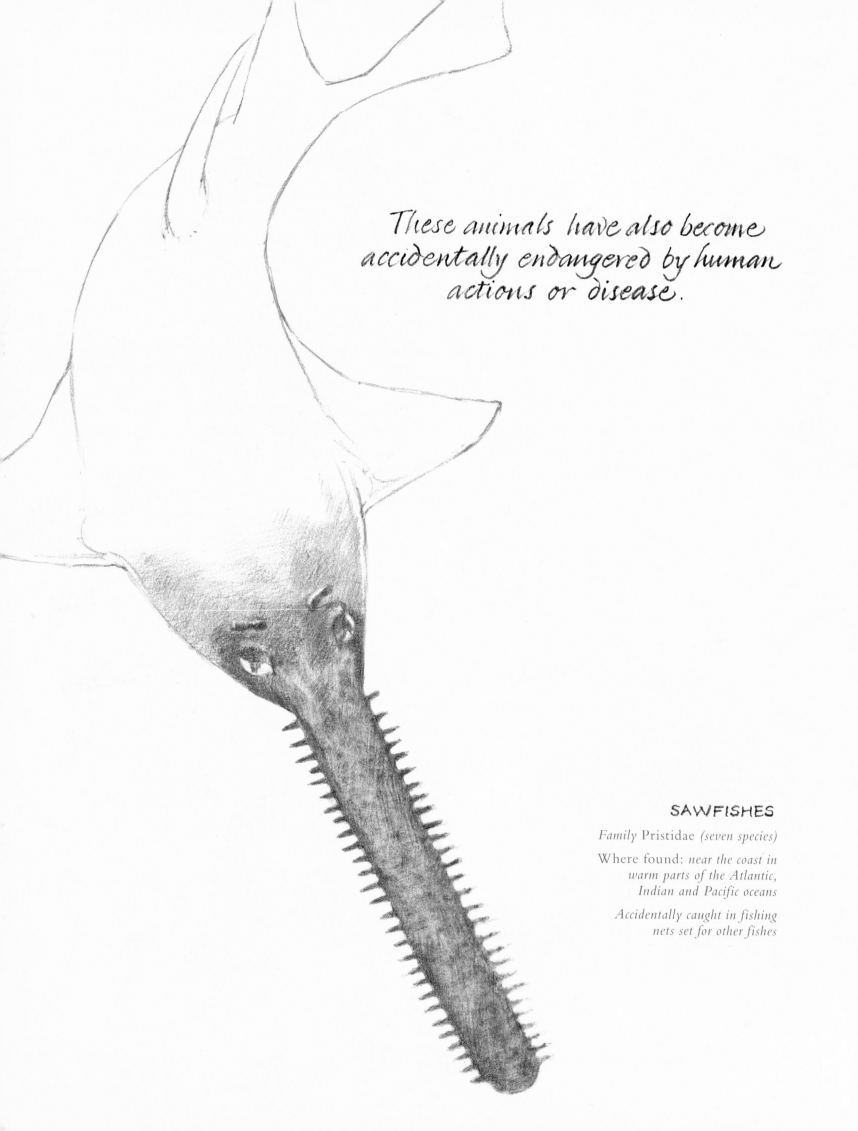

These animals have also become accidentally endangered by human actions or disease.

SAWFISHES

Family Pristidae *(seven species)*

Where found: *near the coast in warm parts of the Atlantic, Indian and Pacific oceans*

Accidentally caught in fishing nets set for other fishes

ALBATROSSES
*Family Diomedeidae
(21 species)*

Where found: *cold
parts of the ocean in the
southern hemisphere*

*Accidentally caught on
fishing hooks set to
catch tuna and
other big fishes*

EUROPEAN CRAYFISH *Astacus astacus*

Where found: *rivers and streams in Europe*

*Affected by crayfish plague caught from
introduced North American crayfish*

**GOLDEN ARROW
POISON FROG**
Atelopus zeteki

Where found: *Panama*

*Affected by a skin disease that people
have probably helped spread*

Sometimes, though, we have managed to do the right thing in time.

There are quite a lot of species that have nearly gone extinct and that we have saved, at least for the time being.

One of these is the American Bison…

AMERICAN BISON *Bison bison*

Where found: *Canada, United States*

Size: *weighs up to 900 kg; measures up to 1.9 m tall at the shoulder and 3.8 m long. Males are bigger than females*

Lifespan: *up to 40 years in zoos; usually 15–20 years in the wild*

Habits: *lives on prairies and in woods. Forms huge herds on prairies but usually lives in small groups in woods*

Breeding: *females have one calf a year. The calf stays with its mother until it is about one year old*

Eats: *grass and other low-growing plants*

Number left: *more than 500,000*

37

The American bison is the biggest land animal in North America. A few hundred years ago there were millions of them roaming the prairies and woodlands. Native people hunted them for their meat and skins, but they didn't kill too many, so there were always plenty around.

Then Europeans arrived with their horses and guns, and things began to change. They killed huge numbers of bison for their skins, they ploughed up parts of the prairies to plant wheat, and they turned the rest into ranches where they could graze cattle. All this left less and less room for the bison. Suddenly there were just two small herds of wild bison left, and a few kept in pens by ranchers. The bison was in danger of becoming extinct, without anyone really noticing.

Luckily, people did begin to take notice. And at the last minute they started to do things.

The ranchers who kept the captive bison started breeding from them, and governments set up reserves to protect the wild herds. Bison numbers began to grow. Now there are hundreds of thousands again. Most of them are still kept by ranchers, who treat them rather like cattle, but there are also some proper wild herds. There are still nowhere near as many as there once were, but there are enough for us not to have to worry about them.

These animals were all once endangered but are now doing well.

WHITE RHINOCEROS
Ceratotherium simum

Where found: *eastern and southern Africa*

Only around 20 survived at the end of the nineteenth century. Now around 17,500

40

VICUÑA *Vicugna vicugna*

Where found: *the Andes Mountains in South America*

Reduced to a few thousand in the 1960s. Now around 350,000

ANTARCTIC FUR SEAL
Arctocephalus gazella

Where found: *cold parts of the ocean in the southern hemisphere*

Nearly extinct at the end of the nineteenth century; now four to six million. Almost all of them breed on South Georgia in the Atlantic Ocean

Bison are actually quite easy animals to look after. As long as you stop hunting them, and make sure they've got a reasonable amount of space, they pretty much take care of themselves.

Not all endangered species are like that. Some you can't take your eye off for a minute. The kakapo is one of these.

Kakapos are amazing birds that live in New Zealand – huge dumpy parrots that can't fly and that only come out at night.

They live as long as people do, they're fussy about what they eat (like a lot of people), and they usually only breed once every three or four years, when their favourite trees produce a bumper crop of fruit or seeds.

KAKAPO *Strigops habroptila*

Where found: *New Zealand*

Size: *weighs up to 4 kg; measures up to 60 cm long*

Lifespan: *probably more than 60 years*

Habits: *lives in woodland and grassland. Feeds at night. Doesn't fly, but jogs along looking for food*

Breeding: *female lays up to three eggs at a time. Only the mother looks after the chicks when they hatch. Chicks stay in the nest until they are 10–12 weeks old*

Eats: *fruit, seeds, flowers, plant shoots and sap from trees*

Number left: *124 (at the last count)*

44

The trouble is that because kakapos can't fly, they are easy prey for animals like rats, dogs, cats and stoats that like to eat them or their eggs. Before people arrived on New Zealand, there were none of these predators there and lots of kakapos. Then, about 1,500 years ago, people started coming, bringing these animals with them, some by accident (like rats) and some on purpose (like dogs and, later, cats and stoats). The kakapos got rarer and rarer. At one point, people thought they might be extinct. Then a handful were discovered in the far south. But there were cats and stoats there too and every year there were fewer kakapos.

Conservationists decided to catch as many of the survivors as possible and put them on small islands, out of reach of predators. That worked, but unfortunately the kakapos hardly ever bred. More were dying, of old age and in accidents, than were hatching out.

By 1995 there were just 51 alive in the world.

Since then people have redoubled their efforts to try to save the kakapo. They guard the islands to make sure no predators arrive. They've put collars with radio transmitters on the kakapos to keep track of them. They've given them extra food to try to persuade them to breed, and when they do breed they keep an eye on the nest using remote-controlled cameras. They've even put heaters over the nests to make sure the eggs or chicks don't get too cold when their mother is off feeding at night. It's all working, and very, very slowly the number of kakapos is growing. By 2010 there were over 120 kakapos – still hardly any, but more than 51.

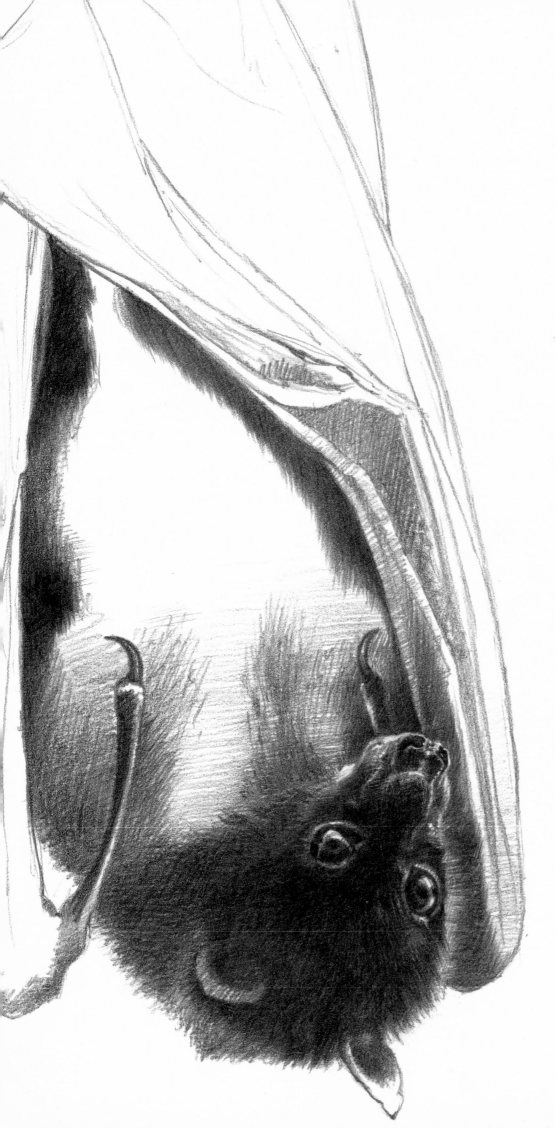

These are some
of the animals
that have been
brought back
from the brink
of extinction
but are still
very rare.

RODRIGUES FLYING FOX
Pteropus rodricensis

Where found:
*Rodrigues Island in
the Indian Ocean.*

*In 1979, only
about 70 survived.
The population reached
5,000 in 2002 but
went down to 4,000 or
so when a cyclone hit
Rodrigues in 2003*

WHOOPING CRANE
Grus americana

Where found: *North America*

*In 1938 only 15 adult birds survived.
By the end of 2007 there were 382 birds
in the wild and 148 in zoos*

BERMUDA CAHOW
Pterodroma cahow

Where found: *Bermuda*

*Thought extinct for 300 years
but rediscovered in the 1950s
breeding on small islands.
Numbers have gone up from
18 pairs in 1951 to around
250 birds now*

49

So you see, trying to save just one endangered species like the kakapo can be hard work, and there are thousands of them altogether. What's more, saving species is going to get more complicated. We haven't just changed the world in obvious ways, like cutting down forests and building roads, we're changing the climate too. And that affects everything, everywhere.

Because of climate change, places like the Arctic that haven't been affected very much by people up till now are starting to change fast, and that means that some animals that we thought were safe – like polar bears – will probably soon be in trouble.

When it comes to looking after all the species that are already endangered, there's such a lot to do that sometimes it might all seem to be too much, especially when there are so many other important things to worry about. But if we stop trying, the chances are that pretty soon we'll end up with a world where there are no tigers or elephants, or sawfishes or whooping cranes, or albatrosses or ground iguanas. Or … I could go on and on.

And I think that would be a shame, don't you?

POLAR BEAR
Ursus maritimus

Where found: *Arctic region of Canada, Greenland, Norway, Russian Federation, USA*

Number left: *20–25,000*

Find out more online

Scientists and conservationists have made a list of about 17,000 animals and plants that they think are in danger. The list includes one in five of all the world's mammals and nearly one in three of all amphibians.

You can find the list, together with extra information about where the species live and why they are endangered, on the website **www.iucnredlist.org.**

The website **www.arkive.org** also has information on a lot of endangered species, including pictures and some great video-clips.

Organizations around the world are working to protect endangered species. They all have websites that tell you what they're up to. Here are some of them:

BirdLife International: **www.birdlife.org**
Conservation International: **www.conservation.org**
Durrell Wildlife Conservation Trust: **www.durrell.org**
Fauna and Flora International: **www.fauna-flora.org**
International Union for Conservation of Nature (IUCN): **www.iucn.org**
Nature Conservancy: **www.nature.org**
Wildlife Conservation Society: **www.wcs.org**
World Wildlife Fund:**www.wwf.org**

Index

About the creators of this book

Martin Jenkins and **Vicky White** are both passionate about conservation.

Martin's first ever job was to help write the IUCN *Red Data Book of Threatened Mammals*. As well as writing books, he is a consultant for the World Conservation Monitoring Centre, working on finding ways to help people conserve wildlife. He's travelled to many parts of the world, like Borneo, Kenya and Madagascar, doing this.

Vicky loves animals and was a zookeeper for six years. She's travelled in India and Africa, drawing and painting animals in the wild. "Coming face to face with a sloth bear or wandering through a troupe of gelada baboons are moments I live for," she says.

Can We Save the Tiger? is the second book Martin and Vicky have made together. Their first was ***Ape***.

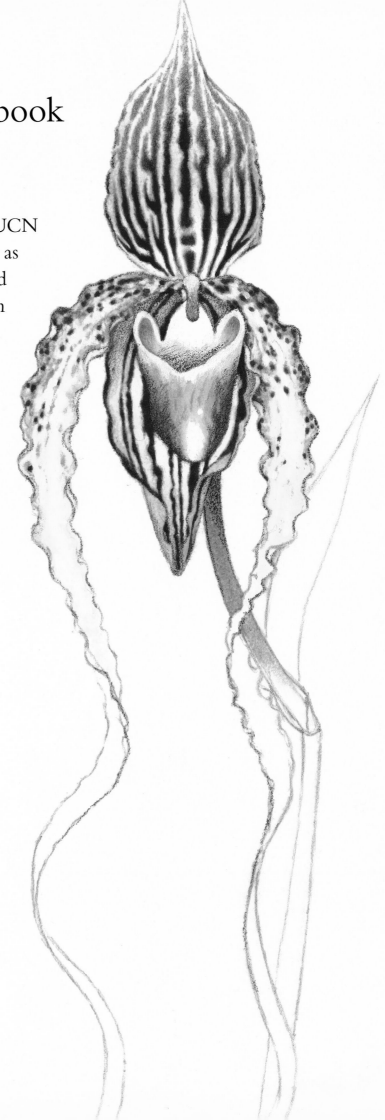

SANDER'S SLIPPER ORCHID
Paphiopedilum sanderianum

Where found: *Sarawak, northwestern Borneo*

Discovered in 1885; thought extinct until rediscovered in 1978. Still very rare, but protected in a national park

Also by Martin Jenkins and Vicky White:

ISBN 978-1-4063-1929-3

"Children wanting to see how monkeys behave in real life should also enjoy *Ape* …
wonderfully illustrated by Vicky White" *Independent*

"expressive faces and fur so detailed you almost feel you could stroke it…
A lovely book for sharing" *Books for Keeps*

"Wonderful … thought-provoking … stunning" *School Librarian*

Winner of the 2008 Key Stage 1 English 4-11 Book Award
Shortlisted for a 2008 Booktrust Early Years Award

Available from all good booksellers

www.walker.co.uk